Contents

Introduction

Japanese legends are full of shape-shifting monsters, and now they can come adorably to life through the art of crochet! This inspirational collection of 12 quirky designs shows you how to create a whole host of lovable monster characters. Each project has clear instructions and colour photographs to help you achieve perfect results. And if you're new to crochet, there's a handy techniques section that explains all the basic skills needed.

Hogaraga

YOU WILL NEED

- Debbie Bliss Cashmerino Aran 55% merino wool, 33% microfibre, 12% cashmere (98yd/90m per 50g): 50g blue, 10g red, 10g orange, 10g yellow, 10g green, 10g pink

- 3.5mm (UK9:USE/4) crochet hook
- 2 blue buttons (for eyes)
- Small pieces of felt (light pink for face and dark pink for mouth)
- Embroidery thread (blue for face, white for toes)
- Polyester stuffing

BODY
Use blue

Round 1: Using magic circle technique (see page 42), work 5 dc. (5 sts).

Round 2: 2dc into each st. (10 sts).

Round 3: (2dc in next dc, dc in next dc) to end. (15 sts).

Round 4: (2dc in next dc, dc in next 2 dc) to end. (20 sts).

Round 5: (2dc in next dc, dc in next 3 dc) to end. (25 sts).

Round 6: (2dc in next dc, dc in next 4 dc) to end. (30 sts).

Round 7: (2dc in next dc, dc in next 5 dc) to end. (35 sts).

Round 8: (2dc in next dc, dc in next 6 dc) to end. (40 sts).

Round 9: Dc to end. (40 sts).

Round 10: (2dc in next dc, dc in next 9 dc) to end. (44 sts).

Round 11: Dc to end. (44 sts).

Round 12: (2dc in next dc, dc in next 10 dc) to end. (48 sts).

Rounds 13–21: Dc to end. (48 sts).

Round 22: (Dc in next 22 dc, dc2tog) to end. (46 sts).

Round 23: Dc to end. (46 sts).

Round 24: Dc2tog once, then to end. (45 sts).

Round 25: (Dc in next 7 dc, dc2tog) to end. (40 sts).

Round 26: (Dc in next 3 dc, dc2tog) to end. (32 sts).

Break off the yarn. Fasten off the work, leaving a tail for sewing. Sew on the eyes with blue embroidery thread and embroider the face and mouth using darned lines. Stuff the body firmly.

Round 27: (Dc in next 2dc, dc2tog) to end. (24 sts).

Round 28: (Dc in next 2dc, dc2tog) to end. (18 sts).

Round 29: (Dc2tog) to end. (9 sts).

Round 30: Dc in first st, then (dc2tog) to end. (5 sts).

Close the hole and hide the tail of the yarn (see page 47).

LEGS
(make 2 alike)

Note: Stuff the leg lightly as it is formed.

Start with blue

Round 1: Using magic circle technique, work 4 dc. (4 sts).

Round 2: 2dc into each st. (8 sts).

Round 3: (2dc in next dc, dc in next dc) to end. (12 sts).

Round 4: (2dc in next dc, dc in next 5 dc) to end. (14 sts).

Rounds 5–6: Dc to end. (14 sts).

Round 7: (Dc in next 5dc, dc2tog) to end. (12 sts).

Round 8: (Dc in next 4dc, dc2tog) to end. (10 sts).

Round 9: Dc to end. (10 sts).

Round 10: (Dc in next 3 dc, dc2tog) to end. (8 sts).

Embroider on the toes with white embroidery thread using darned lines. Stuff the piece and continue to stuff as the leg lengthens.

Rounds 11–13: (Dc to end) in red.

Rounds 14–16: (Dc to end) in orange.

Rounds 17–19: (Dc to end) in yellow.

Rounds 20–22: (Dc to end) in green.

Rounds 23–25: (Dc to end) in blue.

Once the blue rounds have been worked, fasten off and sew to the base of the body.

ARMS
(make 2 alike)
Note: Stuff the arm lightly as it is formed.

Start with pink
Round 1: Using magic circle technique, work 4 dc. (4 sts).
Round 2: 2dc into each st. (8 sts).
Rounds 3–6: Dc to end. (8 sts).

Change to blue
Rounds 7–20: Dc to end. (8 sts).
Break off the yarn. Fasten off the work, leaving a tail for sewing. Sew the arms in place on the body.

MAKING UP
Sew in any loose ends.

BODY

Round	Stitches	Colour
1	MC 5	Blue
2	10 (inc 5)	Blue
3	15 (inc 5)	Blue
4	20 (inc 5)	Blue
5	25 (inc 5)	Blue
6	30 (inc 5)	Blue
7	35 (inc 5)	Blue
8	40 (inc 5)	Blue
9	40	Blue
10	44 (inc 4)	Blue
11	44	Blue
12	48 (inc 4)	Blue
13–21	48	Blue
22	46 (dec 2)	Blue
23	46	Blue
24	45 (dec 1)	Blue
25	40 (dec 5)	Blue
26	32 (dec 8)	Blue

Sew on face, eyes and mouth
Stuff firmly

Round	Stitches	Colour
27	24 (dec 8)	Blue
28	18 (dec 6)	Blue
29	9 (dec 9)	Blue
30	4 (dec 5)	Blue

LEGS

Round	Stitches	Colour
1	MC 4	Blue
2	8 (inc 4)	Blue
3	12 (inc 4)	Blue
4	14 (inc 2)	Blue
5–6	14	Blue
7	12 (dec 2)	Blue
8	10 (dec 2)	Blue
9	10	Blue
10	8 (dec 2)	Blue

Embroider on toes
Stuff as leg continues to lengthen

Round	Stitches	Colour
11–13	8	Red
14–16	8	Orange
17–19	8	Yellow
20–22	8	Green
23–25	8	Blue

ARMS

Round	Stitches	Colour
1	MC 4	Pink
2	8 (inc 4)	Pink
3–6	8	Pink
7–20	8	Blue

Kitsu

YOU WILL NEED

- Debbie Bliss Cashmerino Aran 55% merino wool, 33% microfibre, 12% cashmere (98yd/90m per 50g): 50g orange, 10g red, 15g yellow, 10g pink
- 3.5mm (UK9:USE/4) crochet hook
- 3 turquoise buttons (for eyes)
- Small pieces of felt (white for teeth, black for eyebrows and mouth)
- Embroidery thread (white for teeth, black for eyebrows and mouth)
- Polyester stuffing

EYE BACKINGS
Make 1 each in red, yellow and pink

Round 1: Using magic circle technique (see page 42), work 5 dc. (5 sts).

Round 2: 2dc into each st. (10 sts).

Round 3: (2dc in next dc, dc in next 4 dc) to end. (12 sts).

Rounds 4–10: Dc to end. (12 sts).

Fasten off the work. Break off the yarn, leaving a tail for sewing. Sew on one button eye to each eye backing using orange yarn. Stuff the backings firmly.

HEAD
Use orange

Round 1: Using magic circle technique, work 6 dc. (6 sts).

Round 2: 2dc into each st. (12 sts).

Round 3: (2dc in next dc, dc in next dc) to end. (18 sts).

Round 4: (2dc in next dc, dc in next 2 dc) to end. (24 sts).

Round 5: (2dc in next dc, dc in next 3 dc) to end. (30 sts).

Round 6: (2dc in next dc, dc in next 4 dc) to end. (36 sts).

Round 7: Dc to end. (36 sts).

Round 8: (2dc in next dc, dc in next 17 dc) to end. (38 sts).

Rounds 9–27: Dc around. (38 sts).

Round 28: (Dc in next 17 dc, dc2tog) to end. (36 sts).

Round 29: Dc to end. (36 sts).

Round 30: (Dc in next 4 dc, dc2tog) to end. (30 sts).

Round 31: (Dc in next 3 dc, dc2tog) to end. (24 sts).

Stuff the head firmly.

Round 32: (Dc in next 2 dc, dc2tog) to end. (18 sts).

Round 33: (Dc in next dc, dc2tog) to end. (12 sts).

Round 34: (Dc2tog) to end. (6 sts).

Fasten off the work. Break off the yarn, leaving a tail for sewing. Thread the end through rem sts, then pull tight and secure with a knot. Hide the tail of the yarn (see page 47).

Sew the yellow eye backing to the middle of the head piece and sew the red and pink eye backings to either side of the yellow one with matching yarns.

Sew on the felt mouth and eyebrows with black embroidery thread and the teeth with white embroidery thread using running stitch (see page 47).

FEET
(make 4)
Start with yellow

Round 1: Using magic circle technique, work 6 dc. (6 sts).

Round 2: 2dc into each st. (12 sts).

Round 3: (2dc in next dc, dc in next dc) to end. (18 sts).

Change to orange

Round 4: (Dc in next dc, dc2tog) to end. (12 sts).

Rounds 5–6: Dc to end. (12 sts).

Fasten off the work. Break off the yarn, leaving a tail for sewing. Thread the end through rem sts, then pull tight and secure with a knot. Hide the tail of the yarn (see page 47). Stuff the feet firmly and sew them to the head.

MAKING UP

Weave in any loose ends.

EYE BACKINGS

Round	Stitches	Colour
1	MC 5	Red/Yellow/Pink
2	10 (inc 5)	Red/Yellow/Pink
3	12 (inc 2)	Red/Yellow/Pink
4–10	12	Red/Yellow/Pink

FEET

Round	Stitches	Colour
1	MC 6	Yellow
2	12 (inc 6)	Yellow
3	18 (inc 6)	Yellow
4	12 (dec 6)	Orange
5–6	12	Orange

HEAD

Round	Stitches	Colour
1	MC 6	Orange
2	12 (inc 6)	Orange
3	18 (inc 6)	Orange
4	24 (inc 6)	Orange
5	30 (inc 6)	Orange
6	36 (inc 6)	Orange
7	36	Orange
8	38 (inc 2)	Orange
9–27	38	Orange
28	36 (dec 2)	Orange
29	36	Orange
30	30 (dec 6)	Orange
31	24 (dec 6)	Orange
	Stuff firmly	
32	18 (dec 6)	Orange
33	12 (dec 6)	Orange
34	6 (dec 6)	Orange

Happimon

YOU WILL NEED

- Debbie Bliss Cashmerino Aran 55% merino wool, 33% microfibre, 12% cashmere (98yd/90m per 50g): 25g light blue, 25g dark blue
- 3.5mm (UK9:USE/4) crochet hook
- 2 black buttons (for eyes)
- Small square of black felt (for skull logo)
- Embroidery thread (black for mouth, blue for talons, white for sewing on button eyes and skull detail)
- Polyester stuffing

HEAD
Start with light blue

Round 1: Using magic circle technique (see page 42), work 6 dc. (6 sts).

Round 2: 2dc into each st. (12 sts).

Round 3: (2dc in next dc, dc in next dc) to end. (18 sts).

Round 4: (2dc in next dc, dc in next 2 dc) to end. (24 sts).

Round 5: (2dc in next dc, dc in next 3 dc) to end. (30 sts).

Round 6: (2dc in next dc, dc in next 4 dc) to end. (36 sts).

Round 7: (2dc in next dc, dc in next 5 dc) to end. (42 sts).

Round 8: (2dc in next dc, dc in next 6 dc) to end. (48 sts).

Round 9: Into back loop: dc to end. (48 sts).

Rounds 10–14: Dc to end. (48 sts).

Change to dark blue

Rounds 15–16: Dc to end. (48 sts).

Change to light blue

Rounds 17–19: Dc to end. (48 sts).

Round 20: Into back loop: dc to end. (48 sts).

Round 21: (Dc in next 6dc, dc2tog) to end. (42 sts).

Sew on the eyes with the white embroidery thread and embroider the mouth with the black thread using darned lines as shown.

Round 22: (Dc in next 5 dc, dc2tog) to end. (36 sts).

Round 23: (Dc in next 4 dc, dc2tog) to end. (30 sts).

Round 24: (Dc in next 3 dc, dc2tog) to end. (24 sts).

Fasten off the work. Break off the yarn, leaving a tail for sewing, then stuff the head.

HORNS
(make 2 alike)
Use dark blue

Round 1: Using magic circle technique, work 4 dc. (4 sts).

Round 2: 2dc into each st. (8 sts).

Rounds 3–5: Dc to end. (8 sts).

Round 6: 2dc in next dc, dc in rem dc. (9 sts).

Round 7: Dc to end. (9 sts).

Fasten off the work. Break off the yarn, leaving a tail for sewing. Stuff the horns, then sew them onto the head.

BODY
Use dark blue

Round 1: Using magic circle technique, work 6 dc. (6 sts).

Round 2: 2dc into each st. (12 sts).

Round 3: (2dc in next dc, dc in next dc) to end. (18 sts).

Round 4: (2dc in next dc, dc in next 2 dc) to end. (24 sts).

Rounds 5–10: Dc to end. (24 sts).

Cut a skull shape from felt and sew onto the body with white embroidery thread. Stuff the body, then sew the head to the body.

LEGS
(make 2 alike)
Start with dark blue

Round 1: Using magic circle technique, work 5 dc. (5 sts).

Round 2: 2dc into each st. (10 sts).

Round 3: (2dc in next dc, dc in next dc) to end. (15 sts).

Round 4: (2dc in next dc, dc in next 2 dc) to end. (20 sts).

Rounds 5–6: Dc to end. (20 sts).

Round 7: (Dc in next 2dc, dc2tog) to end. (15 sts).

Round 8: (Dc in next dc, dc2tog) to end. (10 sts).

Partially stuff the legs.

Change to light blue

Rounds 9–13: Dc to end. (10 sts).

Fasten off the work. Break off the yarn, leaving a tail for sewing. Finish stuffing the legs, then attach them to the body.

ARMS
(make 2 alike)
Use light blue

Round 1: Using magic circle technique, work 5 dc. (5 sts).

Round 2: 2dc into each st. (10 sts).

Rounds 3–5: Dc to end. (10 sts).

Round 6: Dc2tog, dc around rem sts. (9 sts).

Round 7: Dc2tog, dc around rem sts. (8 sts).

Round 8: Dc2tog, dc around rem sts. (7 sts).

Round 9: Dc2tog, dc around rem sts. (6 sts).

Fasten off the work.

Break off yarn, leaving a tail for sewing. Stuff the arms, then attach them to the body.

MAKING UP

Embroider the talons with blue embroidery thread using darned lines as shown. Weave in any loose ends.

HEAD

Round	Stitches	Colour
1	MC 6	Light blue
2	12 (inc 6)	Light blue
3	18 (inc 6)	Light blue
4	24 (inc 6)	Light blue
5	30 (inc 6)	Light blue
6	36 (inc 6)	Light blue
7	42 (inc 6)	Light blue
8	48 (inc 6)	Light blue
9	Into back loops 48	Light blue
10–14	48	Light blue
15–16	48	Dark blue
17–19	48	Light blue
20	Into back loops 48	Light blue
21	42 (dec 6)	Light blue
Sew on eyes, embroider mouth		
22	36 (dec 6)	Light blue
23	30 (dec 6)	Light blue
24	24 (dec 6)	Light blue

BODY

Round	Stitches	Colour
1	MC 6	Dark blue
2	12 (inc 6)	Dark blue
3	18 (inc 6)	Dark blue
4	24 (inc 6)	Dark blue
5–10	24	Dark blue

LEGS

Round	Stitches	Colour
1	MC 5	Dark blue
2	10 (inc 5)	Dark blue
3	15 (inc 5)	Dark blue
4	20 (inc 5)	Dark blue
5–6	20	Dark blue
7	15 (dec 5)	Dark blue
8	10 (dec 5)	Dark blue
Partially stuff		
9–13	10	Light blue

HORNS

Round	Stitches	Colour
1	MC 4	Dark blue
2	8 (inc 4)	Dark blue
3–5	8	Dark blue
6	9 (inc 1)	Dark blue
7	9	Dark blue

ARMS

Round	Stitches	Colour
1	MC 5	Light blue
2	10 (inc 5)	Light blue
3–5	10	Light blue
6	9 (dec 1)	Light blue
7	8 (dec 1)	Light blue
8	7 (dec 1)	Light blue
9	6 (dec 1)	Light blue

Hulahulamon

YOU WILL NEED

- Debbie Bliss Cashmerino Aran
  55% merino wool, 33% microfibre,
  12% cashmere (98yd/90m per
  50g) 50g green, 15g orange,
  10g red
- 3.5mm (UK9:USE/4)
  crochet hook
- 2 yellow buttons (for eyes)
- Small piece of felt (red for
  eye mask)
- Embroidery thread (black for
  eyes, eyebrows and mouth)
- Polyester stuffing

BODY
Use green
Round 1: Using magic circle technique (see page 42), work 5 dc. (5 sts).
Round 2: 2dc into each st. (10 sts).
Round 3: (2dc in next dc, dc in next dc) to end. (15 sts).
Round 4: (2dc in next dc, dc in next 2 dc) to end. (20 sts).
Round 5: (2dc in next dc, dc in next 3 dc) to end. (25 sts).
Round 6: (2dc in next dc, dc in next 4 dc) to end. (30 sts).
Round 7: (2dc in next dc, dc in next 5 dc) to end. (35 sts).
Round 8: (2dc in next dc, dc in next 6 dc) to end. (40 sts).
Round 9: (2dc in next dc, dc in next 7 dc) to end. (45 sts).
Round 10: Dc to end. (45 sts).
Round 11: (2dc in next dc, dc in next 8 dc) to end. (50 sts).
Rounds 12–16: Dc to end. (50 sts).
Round 17: (Dc in next 8 dc, dc2tog) to end. (45 sts).
Round 18: Dc to end. (45 sts).
Round 19: (Dc in next 7 dc, dc2tog) to end. (40 sts).
Round 20: (Dc in next 6 dc, dc2tog) to end. (35 sts).

Round 21: (Dc in next 5 dc, dc2tog) to end. (30 sts).
Round 22: (Dc in next 4 dc, dc2tog) to end. (25 sts).
Round 23: Dc to end. (25 sts).
Fill the body with stuffing up to this point (the neck), where the head will be sewn on later.

SKIRT
Use orange
Weave orange yarn around the waist, leaving loops of about 1½in (4cm). Go all the way around the body part and trim loops to the desired skirt length.
Optional: to make it a child-friendly toy, knot the strands to secure in place.

HEAD
Use green
Round 1: Using magic circle technique, work 5 dc. (5 sts).
Round 2: 2 dc into each st. (10 sts).
Round 3: (2dc in next dc, dc in next dc) to end. (15 sts).
Round 4: (2dc in next dc, dc in next 2 dc) to end. (20 sts).
Round 5: (2dc in next dc, dc in next 3 dc) to end. (25 sts).
Round 6: (2dc in next dc, dc in next 4 dc) to end. (30 sts).

Round 7: Dc to end. (30 sts).
Round 8: (Dc in next 4 dc, dc2tog) to end. (25 sts).
Rounds 9–12: Dc to end. (25 sts).

INTERIM FINISHING
Sew on the eyes, eye mask, mouth and eyebrows with black embroidery thread. Stuff the head and sew onto the body.

ARMS
(make 2 alike)
Start with red
Round 1: Using magic circle technique, work 5 dc. (5 sts).
Round 2: 2 dc into each st. (10 sts).
Rounds 3–5: Dc to end. (10 sts).

Change to green
Rounds 6–10: Dc to end. (10 sts).

LEGS
(make 2 alike)
Use red
Round 1: Using magic circle technique, work 6 dc. (6 sts).
Round 2: 2 dc into each st. (12 sts).
Rounds 3–5: Dc to end. (12 sts).

MAKING UP
Sew the arms and legs to the body. Weave in any loose ends.

BODY

Round	Stitches	Colour
1	MC 5	Green
2	10 (inc 5)	Green
3	15 (inc 5)	Green
4	20 (inc 5)	Green
5	25 (inc 5)	Green
6	30 (inc 5)	Green
7	35 (inc 5)	Green
8	40 (inc 5)	Green
9	45 (inc 5)	Green
10	45	Green
11	50 (inc 5)	Green
12–16	50	Green
17	45 (dec 5)	Green
18	45	Green
19	40 (dec 5)	Green
20	35 (dec 5)	Green
21	30 (dec 5)	Green
22	25 (dec 5)	Green
23	25	Green

HEAD

Round	Stitches	Colour
1	MC 5	Green
2	10 (inc 5)	Green
3	15 (inc 5)	Green
4	20 (inc 5)	Green
5	25 (inc 5)	Green
6	30 (inc 5)	Green
7	30	Green
8	25 (dec 5)	Green
9–12	25	Green

ARMS

Round	Stitches	Colour
1	MC 5	Red
2	10 (inc 5)	Red
3–5	10	Red
6–10	10	Green

LEGS

Round	Stitches	Colour
1	MC 6	Red
2	12 (inc 6)	Red
3–5	12	Red

Kaibutsu

BODY
Use pink

Round 1: Using magic circle technique (see page 42), work 6 dc. (6 sts).

Round 2: 2dc into each st. (12 sts).

Round 3: (2dc in next dc, dc in next dc) repeat around. (18 sts).

Round 4: (2dc in next dc, dc in next 2 dc) to end. (24 sts).

Round 5: (2dc in next dc, dc in next 3 dc) to end. (30 sts).

Round 6: (2dc in next dc, dc in next 4 dc) to end. (36 sts).

Round 7: (2dc in next dc, dc in next 5 dc) to end. (42 sts).

Round 8: (2dc in next dc, dc in next 6 dc) to end. (48 sts).

Round 9: (2dc in next dc, dc in next 7 dc) to end. (54 sts).

Rounds 10–12: Dc to end. (54 sts).

Round 13: (Dc in next 4 dc, dc2tog) to end. (45 sts).

Round 14: Dc around. (45 sts).

Round 15: (Dc in next 7 dc, dc2tog) to end. (40 sts).

Round 16: Dc around. (40 sts).

Round 17: (Dc in next 9 dc, dc2tog) to end. (36 sts).

Round 18: Dc to end. (36 sts).

Round 19: (Dc in next 7 dc, dc2tog) to end. (32 sts).

Round 20: Dc to end. (32 sts).

Round 21: (Dc in next 14 dc, dc2tog) to end. (30 sts).

Rounds 22–24: Dc to end. (30 sts).

Round 25: (Dc in next 13 dc, dc2tog) to end. (28 sts).

Rounds 26–28: Dc to end. (28 sts). Sew on mouth and teeth with black embroidery thread using running stitch (see page 47). Stuff firmly.

Round 29: (Dc in next 2 dc, dc2tog) to end. (21 sts).

Round 30: (Dc in next dc, dc2tog) to end. (14 sts).

Embroider the tummy stitching with black embroidery thread as shown.

Round 31: (Dc2tog) to end. (7 sts).

Round 32: (D2tog) to last st, 1 dc. (4 sts). Fasten off the work. Break off the yarn, leaving a tail for sewing. Thread the end through rem sts, then pull tight and secure with a knot. Hide the tail of the yarn (see page 47).

EYE BACKINGS
(make 2 alike)
Use pink

Round 1: Using magic circle technique, work 4 dc. (4 sts).

Round 2: 2dc into each st. (8 sts).

Round 3: (2dc in next dc, dc in next dc) to end. (12 sts).

Round 4: (2dc in next dc, dc in next 2 dc) to end. (16 sts).

Round 5: (2dc in next dc, dc in next 3 dc) to end. (20 sts).

Rounds 6–8: Dc to end. (20 sts).

Round 9: (Dc in next 3 dc, dc2tog) to end. (16 sts).

Sew on button eyes to each eye backing with white embroidery thread. Stuff eye backings, then sew them to the body.

ARMS
(make 2 alike)
Start with white

Round 1: Using magic circle technique, work 8 dc. (8 sts).

Rounds 2–3: Dc to end. (8 sts).

Change to pink

Rounds 4–8: Dc to end. (8 sts). Fasten off the work. Break off the yarn, leaving a tail for sewing. Thread the end through rem sts, then pull tight and secure with a knot. Hide the tail of the yarn (see page 47). Sew the arms to the body.

LEGS
(make 2 alike)
Use black

Round 1: Using magic circle technique, work 6 dc. (6 sts).

Round 2: 2dc into each st. (12 sts).

Rounds 3–7: Dc to end. (12 sts). Fasten off the work. Break off the yarn, leaving a tail for sewing. Thread the end through rem sts, then pull tight and secure with a knot. Hide the tail of the yarn (see page 47). Sew the legs to the body.

MAKING UP
Weave in any loose ends.

BODY

Round	Stitches	Colour
1	MC 6	Pink
2	12 (inc 6)	Pink
3	18 (inc 6)	Pink
4	24 (inc 6)	Pink
5	30 (inc 6)	Pink
6	36 (inc 6)	Pink
7	42 (inc 6)	Pink
8	48 (inc 6)	Pink
9	54 (inc 6)	Pink
10–12	54	Pink
13	45 (dec 9)	Pink
14	45	Pink
15	40 (dec 5)	Pink
16	40	Pink
17	36 (dec 4)	Pink
18	36	Pink
19	32 (dec 4)	Pink
20	32	Pink
21	30 (dec 2)	Pink
22–24	30	Pink
25	28 (dec 2)	Pink
26–28	28	Pink

Sew on mouth and teeth. Stuff firmly

Round	Stitches	Colour
29	21 (dec 7)	Pink
30	14 (dec 7)	Pink

Sew on tummy stitching

Round	Stitches	Colour
31	7 (dec 7)	Pink
32	4 (dec 3)	Pink

Close hole, hide tail

EYE BACKINGS

Round	Stitches	Colour
1	MC 4	Pink
2	8 (inc 4)	Pink
3	12 (inc 4)	Pink
4	16 (inc 4)	Pink
5	20 (inc 4)	Pink
6–8	20	Pink
9	16 (dec 4)	Pink

ARMS

Round	Stitches	Colour
1	MC 8	White
2–3	8	White
4–8	8	Pink

LEGS

Round	Stitches	Colour
1	MC 6	Black
2	12 (inc 6)	Black
3–7	12	Black

Jinkou

YOU WILL NEED

- Debbie Bliss Cashmerino Aran
  55% merino wool, 33% microfibre,
  12% cashmere (98yd/90m per
  50g): 25g purple, 25g pink
- 3.5mm (UK9:USE/4)
  crochet hook

- 2 black buttons (for eyes)
- Small pieces of white felt (for eye
  shapes and nails)
- Embroidery thread (black for nose,
  white for sewing on button eyes)
- Polyester stuffing

HEAD
Start with purple
Round 1: Using magic circle technique (see page 42), work 5 dc. (5 sts).
Round 2: (2dc) into each st. (10 sts).
Round 3: (2dc in next dc, dc in next dc) to end. (15 sts).
Round 4: (2dc in next dc, dc in next 2 dc) to end. (20 sts).
Round 5: (2dc in next dc, dc in next 3 dc) to end. (25 sts).
Round 6: (2dc in next dc, dc in next 4 dc) to end. (30 sts).
Round 7: (2dc in next dc, dc in next 5 dc) to end. (35 sts).
Rounds 8–13: Dc to end. (35 sts).

Change to pink
Rounds 14–16: Dc to end. (35 sts).

Change to purple
Rounds 17–23: Dc to end. (35 sts).
Sew one eye onto the head on top of the felt eye shape with white embroidery thread.
Round 24: (Dc in next 5 dc, dc2tog) to end. (30 sts).
Round 25: (Dc in next 4 dc, dc2tog) to end. (25 sts).
Embroider the nose with black embroidery thread using running stitch (see page 47).
Round 26: (Dc in next 3 dc, dc2tog) to end. (20 sts).
Sew the second eye onto the head on top of the felt eye shape. Partially stuff, then continue stuffing as hole closes.
Round 27: (Dc in next 2 dc, dc2tog) to end. (15 sts).
Round 28: (Dc in next dc, dc2tog) to end. (10 sts).
Round 29: (Dc2tog) to end. (5 sts).
Close the hole and hide the tail of the yarn (see page 47).

ARMS
(make 2 alike)
Start with purple
Round 1: Using magic circle technique, work 7 dc. (7 sts).
Round 2: 2 dc into each st. (14 sts).
Rounds 3–6: Dc to end. (14 sts).
Sew the felt shaped claws onto the arms with white embroidery thread using back stitch.

Change to pink
Round 7: (Dc2tog, then dc in next 5 dc) to end. (12 sts).
Round 8: (Dc2tog, then dc in next 4 dc) to end. (10 sts).
Rounds 9–13: Dc to end. (10 sts).
Secure the tail of yarn and leave.

MAKING UP
Sew the arms to the head using the tail of yarn. Weave in any loose ends.

HEAD

Round	Stitches	Colour
1	MC 5	Purple
2	10 (inc 5)	Purple
3	15 (inc 5)	Purple
4	20 (inc 5)	Purple
5	25 (inc 5)	Purple
6	30 (inc 5)	Purple
7	35 (inc 5)	Purple
8–13	35	Purple
14–16	35	Pink
17–23	35	Purple

Sew one eye on top of felt eye shape

Round	Stitches	Colour
24	30 (dec 5)	Purple
25	25 (dec 5)	Purple
26	20 (dec 5)	Purple

Sew on second eye on top of felt eye shape. Embroider nose. Partially stuff; then cont stuffing as hole closes

Round	Stitches	Colour
27	15 (dec 5)	Purple
28	10 (dec 5)	Purple
29	5 (dec 5)	Purple

Close hole, hide yarn

ARMS

Round	Stitches	Colour
1	MC 7	Purple
2	14 (inc 7)	Purple
3–6	14	Purple

Sew on felt shaped claws

Round	Stitches	Colour
7	12 (dec 2)	Pink
8	10 (dec 2)	Pink
9–13	10	Pink

Hypnomon

YOU WILL NEED

- Debbie Bliss Cashmerino Aran
  55% merino wool, 33% microfibre,
  12% cashmere (98yd/90m per
  50g): 25g blue, 25g white
- 3.5mm (UK9:USE/4)
  crochet hook
- 2 black buttons (for eyeballs)
- Embroidery thread (white for
  sewing on button eyes)
- Polyester stuffing

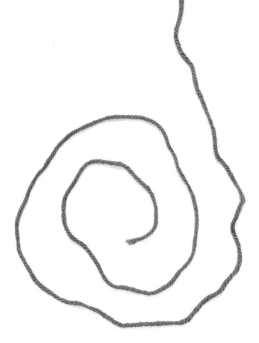

LEGS
(make 2 alike)
Use blue

Round 1: Using magic circle technique, work 5 dc. (5 sts).

Round 2: 2dc into each st. (10 sts).

Rounds 3–10: Dc to end. (10 sts).

Fasten off the work. Break off the yarn, leaving a tail for sewing. Stuff the legs, then sew them to the body.

ARMS
(make 2 alike)
Start with blue

Round 1: Using magic circle technique, work 4 dc. (4 sts).

Round 2: 2 dc into each st. (8 sts).

Round 3: Dc to end. (8 sts).

Change to white

Rounds 4–8: Dc to end. (8 sts).

Fasten off the work. Break off the yarn, leaving a tail for sewing. Stuff the arms, then sew them to the body.

MAKING UP

Weave in any loose ends.

EYE BACKINGS
(make 2 alike)
Use blue

Round 1: Using magic circle technique (see page 42), work 6 dc. (6 sts).

Round 2: 2dc into each st. (12 sts).

Rounds 3–4: Dc to end. (12 sts).

Fasten off the work. Break off the yarn, leaving a tail for sewing. Sew on the buttons for eyeballs.

Lightly stuff the eye backings.

HEAD
Start with white (alternate 2 rounds white with 1 round blue)

Round 1: Using magic circle technique, work 6 dc. (6 sts).

Round 2: 2dc into each st. (12 sts).

Round 3: (2dc in next dc, dc in next dc) to end. (18 sts).

Round 4: (2dc in next dc, dc in next 2 dc) to end. (24 sts).

Round 5: (2dc in next dc, dc in next 3 dc) to end. (30 sts).

Round 6: (2dc in next dc, dc in next 4 dc) to end. (36 sts).

Round 7: (2dc in next dc, dc in next 5 dc) to end. (42 sts).

Round 8: (2dc in next dc, dc in next 6 dc) to end. (48 sts).

Rounds 9–12: Dc to end. (48 sts).

Round 13: (Dc in next 6 dc, dc2tog) to end. (42 sts).

Round 14: (Dc in next 5 dc, dc2tog) to end. (36 sts).

Round 15: (Dc in next 4 dc, dc2tog) to end. (30 sts).

Round 16: (Dc in next 3 dc, dc2tog) to end. (24 sts).

Stuff the head.

Round 17: (Dc in next 2 dc, dc2tog) to end. (18 sts).

Round 18: (Dc in next dc, dc2tog) to end. (12 sts).

Round 19: (Dc2tog) to end. (6 sts).

Round 20: (Dc2tog) to end. (3 sts).

Fasten off the work. Break off the yarn, leaving a tail for sewing. Thread the end through rem sts, then pull tight and secure with a knot. Hide the tail of the yarn (see page 47). Sew the eyes onto the head.

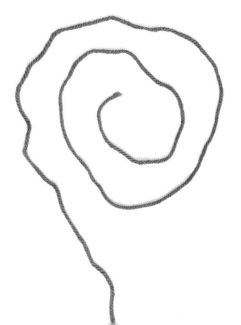

EYE BACKINGS

Round	Stitches	Colour
1	MC 6	Blue
2	12 (inc 6)	Blue
3–4	12	Blue

LEGS

Round	Stitches	Colour
1	MC 5	Blue
2	10 (inc 5)	Blue
3–10	10	Blue

ARMS

Round	Stitches	Colour
1	MC 4	Blue
2	8 (inc 4)	Blue
3	8	Blue
4–8	8	White

HEAD

Round	Stitches	Colour
1	MC 6	White
2	12 (inc 6)	White
3	18 (inc 6)	Blue
4	24 (inc 6)	White
5	30 (inc 6)	White
6	36 (inc 6)	Blue
7	42 (inc 6)	White
8	48 (inc 6)	White
9	48	Blue
10	48	White
11	48	White
12	48	Blue
13	42 (dec 6)	White
14	36 (dec 6)	White
15	30 (dec 6)	Blue
16	24 (dec 6)	White
Stuff		
17	18 (dec 6)	White
18	12 (dec 6)	Blue
19	6 (dec 6)	White
20	3 (dec 3)	White

Hanamono

YOU WILL NEED

- Debbie Bliss Cashmerino Aran 55% merino wool, 33% microfibre, 12% cashmere (98yd/90m per 50g): 50g purple, 15g yellow, 15g orange
- 3.5mm (UK9:USE/4) crochet hook
- 2 yellow buttons (for eyes)
- Small piece of felt (black for eyebrow)
- Embroidery thread (black for eyes)
- Polyester stuffing

HEAD
Use purple

Round 1: Using magic circle technique (see page 42), work 5 dc. (5 sts).

Round 2: 2dc into each st. (10 sts).

Round 3: (2dc in next dc, dc in next dc) to end. (15 sts).

Round 4: (2dc in next dc, dc in next 2 dc) to end. (20 sts).

Round 5: (2dc in next dc, dc in next 3 dc) to end. (25 sts).

Round 6: (2dc in next dc, dc in next 4 dc) to end. (30 sts).

Round 7: (2dc in next dc, dc in next 5 dc) to end. (35 sts).

Round 8: (2dc in next dc, dc in next 6 dc) to end. (40 sts).

Round 9: (2dc in next dc, dc in next 9 dc) to end. (44 sts).

Round 10: (2dc in next dc, dc in next 10 dc) to end. (48 sts).

Rounds 11–23: Dc to end. (48 sts).

Round 24: Working into back loops for this round only, dc to end. (48 sts).

Round 25: (Dc in next 2 dc, dc2tog) to end. (36 sts).

Round 26: (Dc in next 4 dc, dc2tog) to end. (30 sts).

Round 27: (Dc in next dc, dc2tog) to end. (20 sts).

Sew on the button eyes and eyebrow with black embroidery thread. Embroider a mouth with the yellow yarn as shown. Stuff the head firmly.

Round 28: (Dc2tog) to end. (10 sts).

Round 29: (Dc2tog) to end. (5 sts).

Fasten off the work. Break off the yarn, leaving a tail for sewing. Thread the end through rem sts, then pull tight and secure with a knot. Hide the tail of the yarn (see page 47).

PETALS
Make 4 orange and 4 yellow (or enough to alternate around the base of head)

Round 1: Using magic circle technique, work 6 dc. (6 sts).

Round 2: 2dc into each st. (12 sts).

Rounds 3–6: Dc to end. (12 sts).

Fasten off the work. Break off the yarn, leaving a tail for sewing. Sew the petals to the base of the head.

MAKING UP

Weave in any loose ends.

HEAD

Round	Stitches	Colour
1	MC 5	Purple
2	10 (inc 5)	Purple
3	15 (inc 5)	Purple
4	20 (inc 5)	Purple
5	25 (inc 5)	Purple
6	30 (inc 5)	Purple
7	35 (inc 5)	Purple
8	40 (inc 5)	Purple
9	44 (inc 4)	Purple
10	48 (inc 4)	Purple
11–23	48	Purple
24	Into back loops 48	Purple
25	36 (dec 12)	Purple
26	30 (dec 6)	Purple
27	20 (dec 10)	Purple
Sew on eyes, eyebrow and mouth. Stuff firmly		
28	10 (dec 10)	Purple
29	5 (dec 5)	Purple

PETALS

Round	Stitches	Colour
1	MC 6	Orange/Yellow
2	12 (inc 6)	Orange/Yellow
3–6	12	Orange/Yellow

Mokumon

YOU WILL NEED

- Debbie Bliss Cashmerino Aran 55% merino wool, 33% microfibre, 12% cashmere (98yd/90m per 50g): 50g pink
- 3.5mm (UK9:USE/4) crochet hook
- 1 large black button and 1 small yellow button (for eye)
- Small pieces of felt (white for brow and teeth, yellow for nails and mouth)
- Embroidery thread (black for sewing on the button eyes, pink for felt details)
- Polyester stuffing

HEAD AND BODY
Use pink

Round 1: Using magic circle technique (see page 42), work 6 dc. (6 sts).
Round 2: 2dc into each st. (12 sts).
Round 3: (2dc in next dc, dc in next dc) to end. (18 sts).
Round 4: (2dc in next dc, dc in next 2 dc) to end. (24 sts).
Round 5: (2dc in next dc, dc in next 3 dc) to end. (30 sts).
Round 6: (2dc in next dc, dc in next 4 dc) to end. (36 sts).
Round 7: (2dc in next dc, dc in next 5 dc) to end. (42 sts).
Round 8: (2dc in next dc, dc in next 6 dc) to end. (48 sts).
Rounds 9–19: Dc around. (48 sts).
Round 20: (Dc in next 22 dc, dc2tog) to end. (46 sts).
Rounds 21–23: Dc to end. (46 sts).
Round 24: (Dc in next 21 dc, dc2tog) to end. (44 sts).
Round 25: Dc to end. (44 sts).
Round 26: (Dc in next 20 dc, dc2tog) to end. (42 sts).
Round 27: Dc to end. (42 sts).
Round 28: (Dc in next 19 dc, dc2tog) to end. (40 sts).
Round 29: Dc to end. (40 sts).
Round 30: (Dc in next 18 dc, dc2tog) to end. (38 sts).
Round 31: Dc to end. (38 sts).
Round 32: (Dc in next 17 dc, dc2tog) to end. (36 sts).
Round 33: Dc around. (36 sts).
Partially stuff.
Continue from here to begin the legs.

LEGS
Leg A (bigger leg)
Continue in pink

Round 34a: Dc around 24 sts, then join into first st. (24 sts).
Sew on the eye buttons with black embroidery thread and the white and yellow felt for the brow, teeth and mouth with pink embroidery thread using back stitch.
Round 35a: Dc around. (24 sts).
Round 36a: (Dc in next dc, dc2tog) to end. (18 sts).
Round 37a: (Dc in next dc, dc2tog) to end. (12 sts).
Stuff the whole piece firmly.
Round 38a: (Dc2tog) to end. (6 sts).
Round 39a: (Dc2tog) to end. (3 sts).
Fasten off the work. Break off the yarn, leaving a tail for sewing. Close the hole and hide the tail of the yarn (see page 47).

Leg B (smaller leg)
Continue in pink

Round 34b: Dc around rem 12 sts, then join into first st. (12 sts).

Round 35b: Dc to end. (12 sts).
Round 36b: (Dc in next 4 dc, dc2tog) to end. (10 sts).
Round 37b: (Dc in next 3 dc, dc2tog) to end. (8 sts).
Stuff the leg firmly.
Round 38b: (Dc in next 2 dc, dc2tog) to end. (6 sts).
Round 39b: (Dc2tog) to end (3 sts).
Fasten off the work. Break off the yarn, leaving a tail for sewing. Close the hole and hide the tail of the yarn (see page 47).

Arms
(make 2 alike)
Use pink

Round 1: Using magic circle technique, work 4 dc. (4 sts).
Round 2: 2dc into each st. (8 sts).
Rounds 3–7: Dc to end. (8 sts).

MAKING UP

Sew on the felt nails with pink embroidery thread using back stitch and lightly stuff the arms, then sew the arms to the body. Weave in any loose ends.

HEAD AND BODY

Round	Stitches	Colour
1	MC 6	Pink
2	12 (inc 6)	Pink
3	18 (inc 6)	Pink
4	24 (inc 6)	Pink
5	30 (inc 6)	Pink
6	36 (inc 6)	Pink
7	42 (inc 6)	Pink
8	48 (inc 6)	Pink
9–19	48	Pink
20	46 (dec 2)	Pink
21–23	46	Pink
24	44 (dec 2)	Pink
25	44	Pink
26	42 (dec 2)	Pink
27	42	Pink
28	40 (dec 2)	Pink
29	40	Pink
30	38 (dec 2)	Pink
31	38	Pink
32	36 (dec 2)	Pink
33	36	Pink

Partially stuff
Form legs

LEGS

Round	Stitches	Colour
Leg A		
34a	24 – rejoin to first st	Pink
Sew on eye buttons, brow, teeth, mouth and nails		
35a	24	Pink
36a	18 (dec 6)	Pink
37a	12 (dec 6)	Pink
Stuff leg		
38a	6 (dec 6)	Pink
39a	3 (dec 3)	Pink
Leg B		
34b	12 (rejoin to first st)	Pink
35b	12 (dec 2)	Pink
36b	10 (dec 2)	Pink
37b	8 (dec 2)	Pink
Stuff leg		
38b	6 (dec 2)	Pink
39b	3 (dec 3)	Pink

ARMS

Round	Stitches	Colour
1	MC 4	Pink
2	8 (inc 4)	Pink
3–7	8	Pink

Kumomon

YOU WILL NEED

- Debbie Bliss Cashmerino Aran
  55% merino wool, 33% microfibre,
  12% cashmere (98yd/90m
  per 50g): 25g yellow, 15g red,
  10g black
- 3.5mm (UK9:USE/4)
  crochet hook

- 2 black buttons (for eyes)
- Small piece of red felt
  (for eyepiece)
- Embroidery thread (black for
  mouth, white for sewing on
  button eyes)
- Polyester stuffing

HEAD AND EARS
Use yellow

Round 1: Using magic circle technique (see page 42), work 5 dc. (5 sts).

Round 2: 2dc into each st. (10 sts).

Round 3: (2dc in next dc, dc in next dc) to end. (15 sts).

Round 4: (2dc in next dc, dc in next 2 dc) to end. (20 sts).

Round 5: (2dc in next dc, dc in next 3 dc) to end. (25 sts).

Round 6: (2dc in next dc, dc in next 4 dc) to end. (30 sts).

Round 7: (2dc in next dc, dc in next 5 dc) to end. (35 sts).

Round 8: (2dc in next dc, dc in next 6 dc) to end. (40 sts).

Rounds 9–18: Dc to end. (40 sts).

EAR A
Continue in yellow

Round 19a: Dc around 20 sts, then join into first stitch. (20 sts).

Round 20a: Dc to end. (20 sts).

Sew on the felt eyepiece using running stitch (see page 47) or use fabric glue.

Sew on the buttons for the eyes with white embroidery thread.

Embroider the mouth using running stitch with black embroidery thread. Partially stuff the head.

Round 21a: Dc2tog, dc to last 2 sts, dc2tog. (18 sts).

Round 22a: Dc2tog, dc to last 2 sts, dc2tog. (16 sts).

Round 23a: Dc2tog, dc to last 2 sts, dc2tog. (14 sts).

Round 24a: Dc2tog, dc to last 2 sts, dc2tog. (12 sts).

Round 25a: Dc2tog, dc to last 2 sts, dc2tog. (10 sts).

Stuff the head and ears tightly.

Round 26a: Dc2tog, dc to last 2 sts, dc2tog. (8 sts).

Round 27a: Dc2tog, dc to last 2 sts, dc2tog. (6 sts).

Round 28a: Dc2tog, dc to last 2 sts, dc2tog. (4 sts).

Fasten off the work. Break off the yarn, leaving a tail for sewing. Thread the end through rem sts, then pull tight and secure with a knot. Hide the tail of the yarn (see page 47).

EAR B
Continue in yellow

Rejoin the yarn to the middle of the top of the head.

Round 19b: Dc around 20 rem sts of round 18, then join into first stitch. (20 sts).

Round 20b: Dc to end. (20 sts).

Rounds 21b–28b: Work as for rounds 21a–28a and finish off as for ear A.

BODY
Use red

Round 1: Using magic circle technique, work 5 dc. (5 sts).

Round 2: 2dc into each st. (10 sts).

Round 3: (2dc in next dc, dc in next dc) to end. (15 sts).

Round 4: (2dc in next dc, dc in next 2 dc) to end. (20 sts).

Rounds 5–8: Dc to end. (20 sts).

Fasten off the work. Break off the yarn, leaving a tail for sewing. Stuff the body then sew it to the head.

HEAD

Round	Stitches	Colour
1	MC 5	Yellow
2	10 (inc 5)	Yellow
3	15 (inc 5)	Yellow
4	20 (inc 5)	Yellow
5	25 (inc 5)	Yellow
6	30 (inc 5)	Yellow
7	35 (inc 5)	Yellow
8	40 (inc 5)	Yellow
9–18	40	Yellow
Divide for ears		
19a/b–20a/b	20	Yellow
21a/b	18 (dec 2)	Yellow
22a/b	16 (dec 2)	Yellow
23a/b	14 (dec 2)	Yellow
24a/b	12 (dec 2)	Yellow
25a/b	10 (dec 2)	Yellow
Stuff tightly		
26a/b	8 (dec 2)	Yellow
27a/b	6 (dec 2)	Yellow
28a/b	4 (dec 2)	Yellow

BODY

Round	Stitches	Colour
1	MC 5	Red
2	10 (inc 5)	Red
3	15 (inc 5)	Red
4	20 (inc 5)	Red
5–8	20	Red

LEGS

Round	Stitches	Colour
1	MC 6	Black
2–8	6	Black
9–11	6	Red

ARMS

Round	Stitches	Colour
1	MC 6	Red
2–5	6	Red
6–13	6	Yellow

LEGS
(make 2 alike)
Start with black
Round 1: Using magic circle technique, work 6 dc. (6 sts).
Rounds 2–8: Dc to end. (6 sts).

Change to red
Rounds 9–11: Dc to end. (6 sts).
Fasten off the work. Break off the yarn, leaving a tail for sewing. Stuff the legs, then sew them to the body.

ARMS
(make 4 alike)
Start with red
Round 1: Using magic circle technique, work 6 dc. (6 sts).
Rounds 2–5: Dc to end. (6 sts).

Change to yellow
Rounds 6–13: Dc to end. (6 sts).
Fasten off the work. Break off the yarn, leaving a tail for sewing. Stuff the arms, then sew them to the body.

MAKING UP
Weave in any loose ends.

Mono-mono

YOU WILL NEED

- Debbie Bliss Cashmerino Aran 55% merino wool, 33% microfibre, 12% cashmere (98yd/90m per 50g): 50g red, 50g black, 10g blue, 10g pink
- 3.5mm (UK9:USE/4) crochet hook
- 4 black buttons (for eyes)
- Embroidery thread (pink and blue for mouths and sewing on button eyes)
- Polyester stuffing

BODY AND HEADS
Start with black (alternate 2 rows black with 2 rows red)

Round 1: Using magic circle technique (see page 42), work 7 dc. (7 sts).
Round 2: 2dc into each st. (14 sts).
Round 3: (2dc in next dc, dc in next dc) to end. (21 sts).
Round 4: (2dc in next dc, dc in next 2 dc) to end. (28 sts).
Round 5: (2dc in next dc, dc in next 3 dc) to end. (35 sts).
Round 6: (2dc in next dc, dc in next 4 dc) to end. (42 sts).
Round 7: (2dc in next dc, dc in next 5 dc) to end. (49 sts).
Round 8: (2dc in next dc, dc in next 6 dc) to end. (56 sts).
Rounds 9–20: Dc to end. (56 sts). Partially stuff.

Head A
Change to pink for head A

Round 21a: Dc around 28 sts, then join into first stitch. (28 sts).
Rounds 22a–27a: Dc to end. (28 sts). Embroider the mouth as shown with pink and blue embroidery thread.

Round 28a: (Dc in next 5 dc, dc2tog) to end. (24 sts).
Round 29a: (Dc in next 4 dc, dc2tog) to end. (20 sts).
Round 30a: (Dc in next 3 dc, dc2tog) to end. (16 sts).
Sew two buttons onto the head for the eyes with pink and blue embroidery thread to match the colour of the head.
Stuff the head firmly.
Round 31a: (Dc in next 2 dc, dc2tog) to end. (12 sts).
Round 32a: (Dc in next dc, dc2tog) to end. (8 sts).
Round 33a: (Dc2tog) to end. (4 sts).
Fasten off the work. Break off the yarn, leaving a tail for sewing. Thread the end through rem sts, then pull tight and secure with a knot. Hide the tail of the yarn (see page 47).

Head B
Change to blue for head B

Round 21b: Dc around rem 28 sts of round 20, then join into first stitch. (28 sts).
Rounds 22b–33b: Work as for rounds 22a–33a (but using blue).
Finish off as for head A.

ARMS
Arm A
Start with blue

Note: Stuff gradually as arm length grows.
Round 1: Using magic circle technique, work 8 dc. (8 sts).
Rounds 2–5: Dc to end. (8 sts).

Change to red

Rounds 6–7: Dc to end. (8 sts).

Change to black

Rounds 8–27: Dc to end. (8 sts).
Fasten off the work. Break off the yarn, leaving a tail for sewing. Sew the arm to the body.

Arm B
Start with pink

Note: Stuff gradually as arm length grows.
Round 1: Using magic circle technique, work 8 dc. (8 sts).
Rounds 2–5: Dc to end. (8 sts).

Change to black

Rounds 6–7: Dc to end. (8 sts).

Change to red

Rounds 8–27: Dc to end. (8 sts).
Fasten off the work. Break off the yarn, leaving a tail for sewing. Sew the arm to the body.

MAKING UP
Knot strands of yarn to form hair on each head (see page 47) and trim to desired length. Weave in any loose ends.

BODY AND HEADS

Round	Stitches	Colour	
1	MC 7	Black	
2	14 (inc 7)	Black	
3	21 (inc 7)	Red	
4	28 (inc 7)	Red	
5	35 (inc 7)	Black	
6	42 (inc 7)	Black	
7	49 (inc 7)	Red	
8	56 (inc 7)	Red	
9–20	56	2 rounds Black	2 rounds Red
21a/b	28 – rejoin to first st	Head A Pink	Head B Blue
22–27a/b	28		
	Embroider mouth		
28a/b	24 (dec 4)	Head A Pink	Head B Blue
29a/b	20 (dec 4)		
30a/b	16 (dec 4)		
	Sew on eyes, stuff firmly		
31a/b	12 (dec 4)	Head A Pink	Head B Blue
32a/b	8 (dec 4)		
33a/b	4 (dec 4)		

ARM A

Round	Stitches	Colour
1	MC 8	Blue
2–5	8	Blue
6–7	8	Red
8–27	8	Black

ARM B

Round	Stitches	Colour
1	MC 8	Pink
2–5	8	Pink
6–7	8	Black
8–27	8	Red

Punkymon

YOU WILL NEED

- Debbie Bliss Cashmerino Aran
  55% merino wool, 33% microfibre,
  12% cashmere (98yd/90m
  per 50g): 30g blue, 30g red
- 3.5mm (UK9:USE/4)
  crochet hook
- 2 black buttons (for eyes)
- Embroidery thread (white for
  mouth and sewing on button eyes)
- Polyester stuffing

BODY AND LEGS
Start with blue

Round 1: Using magic circle technique (see page 42), work 6 dc. (6 sts).

Round 2: 2dc into each st. (12 sts).

Round 3: (2dc in next dc, dc in next dc) to end. (18 sts).

Round 4: (2dc in next dc, dc in next 2 dc) to end. (24 sts).

Round 5: (2dc in next dc, dc in next 3 dc) to end. (30 sts).

Round 6: (2dc in next dc, dc in next 4 dc) to end. (36 sts).

Round 7: (2dc in next dc, dc in next 5 dc) to end. (42 sts).

Round 8: (2dc in next dc, dc in next 6 dc) to end. (48 sts).

Rounds 9–25: Dc to end. (48 sts).

Change to red

Rounds 26–30: Dc to end. (48 sts). Sew on the buttons for the eyes with the white embroidery thread, and embroider the mouth as shown using running stitch (see page 47).

To form 2 legs (Leg A and Leg B), continue from body part.

Leg A
Continue in red

Round 31a: Dc around 24 sts, then join into first stitch. (24 sts).

Round 32a–34a: Dc to end. (24 sts).

Round 35a: (Dc in next 4 dc, dc2tog) to end. (20 sts).

Round 36a: (Dc in next 3 dc, dc2tog) to end. (16 sts).

Round 37a: (Dc in next 2 dc, dc2tog) to end. (12 sts).

Round 38a: (Dc2tog) to end. (6 sts). Fasten off the work. Break off the yarn, leaving a tail for sewing. Thread the end through rem sts, then pull tight and secure with a knot. Hide the tail of the yarn (see page 47). Stuff the body and leg A.

Leg B
Continue in red

Round 31b: Dc around 24 sts, then join into first stitch. (24 sts).

Rounds 32b–34b: Dc to end. (24 sts).

Round 35b: (Dc in next 4 dc, dc2tog) to end. (20 sts).

Round 36b: (Dc in next 3 dc, dc2tog) to end. (16 sts).

Round 37b: (Dc in next 2 dc, dc2tog) to end. (12 sts).

Round 38b: (Dc2tog) to end. (6 sts). Stuff leg B. Fasten off the work. Break off the yarn, leaving a tail for sewing. Thread the end through rem sts, then pull tight and secure with a knot. Hide the tail of the yarn (see page 47).

MAKING UP

Weave in any loose ends. Using the red yarn, loop and knot to form Mohican hair (see page 47).

BODY AND LEGS

Round	Stitches	Colour
1	MC 6	Blue
2	12 (inc 6)	Blue
3	18 (inc 6)	Blue
4	24 (inc 6)	Blue
5	30 (inc 6)	Blue
6	36 (inc 6)	Blue
7	42 (inc 6)	Blue
8	48 (inc 6)	Blue
9–25	48	Blue
26–30	48	Red
Begin legs		
31a/b	24 – rejoin to first st	Red
32–34a/b	24	Red
35a/b	20 (dec 4)	Red
36a/b	16 (dec 4)	Red
37a/b	12 (dec 4)	Red
38a/b	6 (dec 6)	Red

Stuff and close

Loop and knot yarn to form Mohican hair

What is amigurumi?

The Japanese art of amigurumi is the crocheting or knitting of cute stuffed creatures. The word derives from the Japanese words 'ami', meaning crocheted or knitted, and 'nuigurumi', which means stuffed doll. Amigurumi creatures, such as the ones in this booklet, are made from yarn that is worked with a smaller size of hook than is usual for the weight of yarn. This produces a closely woven fabric without any gaps through which stuffing might escape. Amigurumi are usually worked in sections and joined, though some designs may have a head and torso but no limbs, and be worked in one piece.

The simplest amigurumi designs are worked in spirals, but unlike traditional Western crochet, which is usually made in joined rounds, the various parts are made individually, then stuffed and sewn together. A typical amigurumi toy will consist of an over-sized round head, a cylindrical body, arms and legs, plus ears and tail if appropriate. The body is usually stuffed with fibre stuffing, while limbs and other extremities are sometimes stuffed with plastic pellets to give them a lifelike weight. Safety eyes may be used, or the features may simply be embroidered on the toy.

Felt is often used to create the ears, face, or nose, and it may also be used to make cute embellishments.

CROCHET HOOKS

Traditional crochet hooks range from a bent needle in a cork handle to expensively crafted silver, brass, steel, ivory and bone hooks. Modern hooks are usually made from aluminium, plastic or steel, but are also available in wood and bamboo.

For amigurumi, we recommend aluminium or steel hooks. We often work with pieces that require tight, dense stitches and find metal hooks easier to use as they slip more easily between the stitches. We can also pull on them as much as we like without worrying that they will snap! The obvious disadvantage of metal hooks is that they are cold to the touch and can be very slippery, so choose what you feel comfortable with. For projects that require larger hooks or very thick yarn, it may be worth experimenting with wooden hooks because they are not as slippery as metal hooks and are available in beautiful designs.

Hooks are sized according to thickness, and the size is identified in millimetres or by a letter (US). In this book, we have used a 3.5mm hook, but any size can be used and the choice of yarn adapted accordingly. Remember that the smaller the hook, the tighter and denser the stitches. Tight, dense stitches are what you want to achieve, though not so tight that they are impossible to work! As a rough guide, hooks sized from 3mm to 3.5mm are suitable for most cashmere-mix or acrylic Aran yarn.

Just to make things more interesting, there are different US and UK terms for crochet stitches. This book uses the UK name, double crochet (dc), rather than the US term, single crochet (sc).

CHOOSING YARN

There are three main choices when considering yarn for amigurumi projects: colour, structure and weight. Beside these important choices, we also look at the practical care of your creations.

With children in mind, we have tried to make everything washable and easy to care for, leaving you more time to create more fun projects. We have used Aran-weight yarn. The yarn chosen is durable and gives a solid finish, which helps the completed toy to hold its shape. These yarn types are twisted, so the strands are less likely to unravel, and they are also easier to work when you are using a small hook.

Colour

There are two main approaches to selecting the right colour yarn for your project: by using contrasting colours, or by using complementary colours. Contrasting colours typically work well for 'bold' projects with large pieces to make up and contrast. Complementary colours and softer shades such as pastels work well for more 'delicate' projects and smaller pieces. There are no rights or wrongs, so mix and match as you like to make your work unique, and personalized to your taste.

Colour-fastness

It is a good idea to choose a yarn that is colour-fast, especially if the finished item is intended for a child. Most modern yarn is colour-fast, but yarn produced by traditional dyeing methods may not be. For projects made in multiple shades it is particularly important to test for colour-fastness, to ensure that a dark colour will not run into a pale colour. To test this, simply wet a piece of the yarn, wrap tightly round a piece of white paper towel and leave to dry. Unwind the yarn; if the towel has changed colour, the yarn is not colour-fast and may need to be dry cleaned.

Yarn structure

Yarns are made up of thin strands of spun fibre, twisted together to make up the required thickness. The twist is another important consideration: with some yarns the twist quickly unravels if you make a few mistakes and need to undo and rework. Choose a yarn with a firm twist that is less likely to unravel during the process.

Yarn weight

Yarns are generally classified into different types (see below). We have mainly used medium-weight yarn for our projects.

YARN WEIGHT

Yarn weight	Yarn type
lace	2-ply
super fine	3-ply (US fingering)
fine	4-ply (US sport); sock; lightweight DK
light	DK (US light worsted)
medium	Aran (US fisherman/worsted); Afghan
heavy	Chunky (US bulky)
very heavy	Super chunky (US extra-bulky)

YARN TYPE

The range of available yarns has grown with new technology, which has allowed different fibres to be spun and twisted into yarn. Different fibres have varying properties, so the various yarns will be suitable for different types of projects.

Wool

This warm, breathable natural fibre is very popular. Most wool yarn comes from the fleeces of sheep but is also produced from the wool of some breeds of goat, llama, camel and rabbit. It is very easy to work and its elasticity is useful if your tension is uneven. Care must be taken when washing the finished item, to avoid unexpected 'felted' effects.

Cotton

This plant fibre is available in varying grades of softness. Cotton is very kind to the skin and is suitable for people with skin allergies. It takes dye well, and produces beautiful strong colours. It also washes well.

Silk

This yarn is produced from the cocoons of various kinds of silk moth. Collecting and spinning the silk fibres is a time-consuming job, hence the high cost of silk yarn. Silk-mix yarns may be a cost-effective alternative.

Mixed fibres

Many different textures and weights of yarn are available in a wide range of fibres that are mixed for their different qualities and properties.

Environmentally friendly

Natural fibre yarns, including soya and bamboo, are becoming increasingly popular.

Novelty

These yarns are usually spun from man-made fibres, and are often made up of several plies or strands of yarn that are twisted together.

Other materials

Apart from yarn and hooks, the craft of amigurumi requires relatively few materials. Each project will be an individual creation, and the personalization will come in your finishing touches. Our designs should be regarded as a springboard for your own ideas; with this in mind, these are some of the additional materials you may need.

Stuffing

We used Minicraft Supersoft Toy Stuffing, which conforms to BS1425, BN5852 and EN71 standards and is safe for children. It is washable, can be used in all types of toy making and is readily available in good craft stores as well as online.

Tapestry needle

These have rounded tips and will be used to stitch or join the different parts of your amigurumi. As an alternative to using embellishments, your finished toy may also be embroidered.

Felt

Felt may be used to make eyes and other embellishments for amigurumi. The advantage of felt is that it is available in a wide assortment of colours, so it is ideal for making your project individual. The disadvantage is that the colour may run; if in doubt, check for colour-fastness or use another material. If you want to make a toy that is easily laundered, substitute scraps of any washable fabric as a child-friendly alternative to felt.

Eyes

Many different types of toy eyes are available, including safety eyes that are secured on the inside of the toy using washers, sewn-on eyes and eyes that may be attached using adhesive. Most of the projects in this book use buttons for eyes or have eyes embroidered using embroidery thread. For a more child-friendly version, consider using safety eyes.

Embroidery thread

You will need an assortment of different-coloured threads to add detail to your work. Your creatures may be personalized by embroidering features and patterns and you will discover your creative side as your confidence increases.

Crochet techniques

CHAIN STITCH

1 Form a slip knot on the hook. With the hook in the right hand and yarn resting over the middle finger of the left hand, pull yarn taut. Take the hook under, then over yarn.

2 Pull the hook and yarn through the loop, holding the slip knot steady. Repeat action to form an even chain.

DOUBLE CROCHET

1 Starting with a foundation chain, insert the hook into the next stitch. Wrap the yarn round the hook and draw it back through the stitch; there should now be two loops on the hook.

2 Wrap the yarn round the hook again, then draw it through both loops so there is one loop left on the hook. Repeat across the row.

MAGIC CIRCLE TECHNIQUE

Many crochet patterns begin by working a chain of stitches and linking them in a ring with a slip stitch. This may leave an unsightly hole, depending on how many chain stitches you begin with. For small, neat work like amigurumi, this is not ideal as it may spoil the look of the finished toy.

A better method is to begin by using the magic circle technique, in which stitches are worked over a loop of yarn. The loop is then pulled taut and fastened off, leaving no hole. The step-by-step illustrations here will help you to work your first magic circle.

Practise the magic circle until you feel confident so you can form a good solid foundation ring to build your crochet monster upon. Having a good foundation is important to the success of your crochet.

MAKING THE LOOP

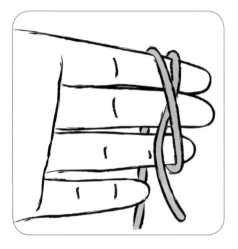

1 Wrap the yarn around your fingers to form a ring.

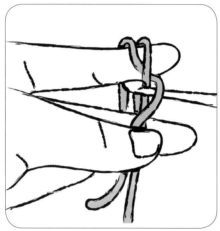

2 Insert the hook and pick up a loop of yarn.

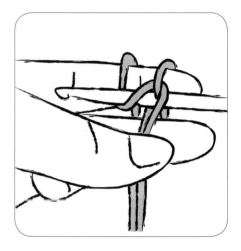

3 Take yarn over hook and pull through to form a loop.

WORKING IN THE RING

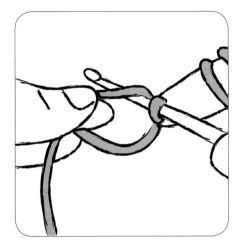

4 Insert the hook into the ring…

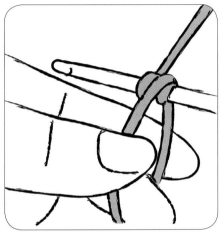

5 …wrap yarn round hook…

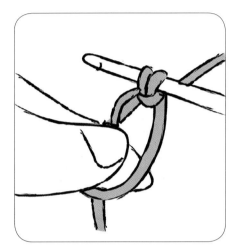

6 …and pull through ring so there are two loops on the hook.

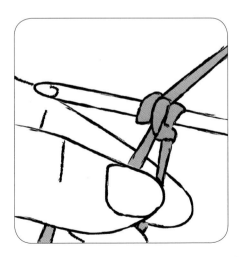

7 Wrap yarn round hook again and pull through both loops…

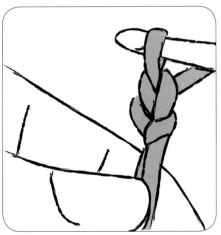

8 …to complete the first dc.

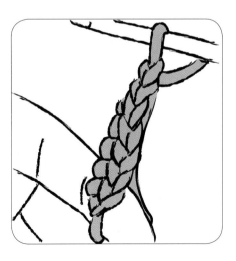

9 Continue in dc round the ring.

CHANGING COLOURS

To ensure a good finish for your creations, it is important to practise changing colours neatly and efficiently. Begin dc in the normal way by inserting the hook into the stitch, then wrapping the yarn round and pulling through.

1 Wrap the second colour round the hook.

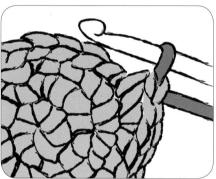

2 Pull through both loops of the first colour. Tie ends to stop them escaping as you work.

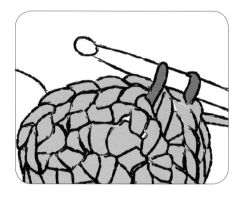

3 Using the second colour of yarn, dc into next stitch.

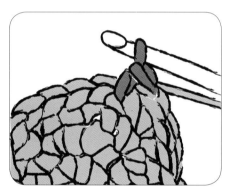

4 Repeat step 3.

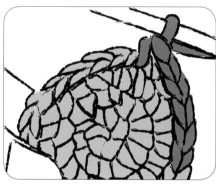

5 The colour change is now complete.

INCREASING AND DECREASING

Increasing

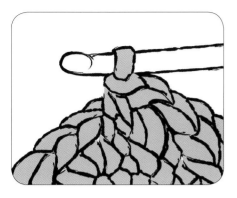

Work 2 dc into the same stitch.

Decreasing

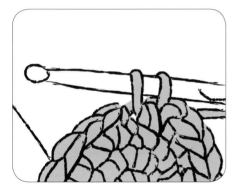

1 Insert hook into stitch, wrap yarn round and pull through.

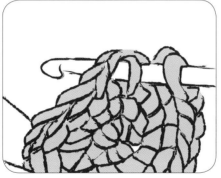

2 Insert hook into next stitch, wrap yarn, and pull through.

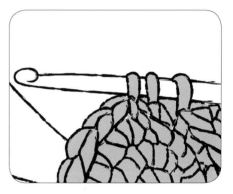

3 The hook should contain three loops.

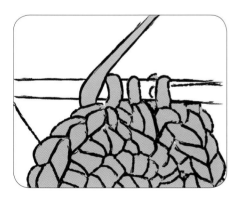

4 Complete the decrease by wrapping yarn around hook and pulling through all three loops…

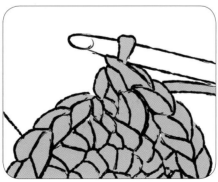

5 …to complete the decrease (also known as 2 sts into 1).

AMIGURUMI SPIRALS

Some amigurumi patterns give the instructions in the form of diagrams showing the spirals to be worked. We think it is easier to work from simple row-by-row charts, so you know exactly where you are at any time, and how many stitches are on each row.

It is easy to count the number of rows that you have worked on any piece of amigurumi: just count the ridges produced by the rows of double-crochet stitches. To determine where a row begins or ends, start with the end of yarn left when making the initial magic circle and count vertically. If you are worried about this, you can use a contrast thread or stitch markers to delineate the beginning of the rows.

This illustration shows how the chart instructions can be rendered as spiral diagrams.

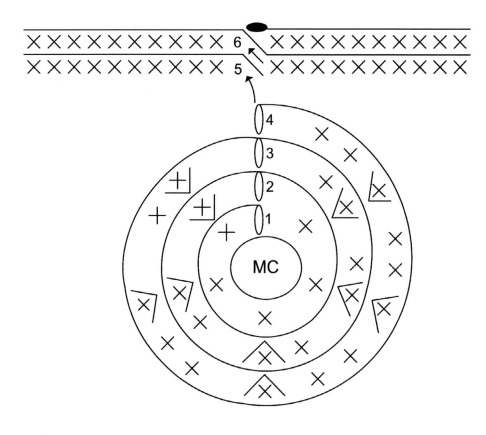

KEY		
Symbol	**UK Term**	**US Term**
✕	dc (double crochet)	sc (single crochet)
⋎	2dc inc	2-sc inc (2 single-crochet increase)

SEWING AND FINISHING TECHNIQUES

Hiding yarn tails

Thread or stitch the tail into a section of the body that is the same colour and then pull out on the other side of the body piece (it's best to squeeze the body piece if the needle is too short). Trim so that the yarn is in line with the body and therefore hidden.

Making hair

Using a needle, thread 2in (5cm) strands of yarn through the stitches on the head or body and knot using an overhand knot. You can use a double overhand knot if you wish, to make it extra secure.

Closing a hole

Finish off a hole by crocheting two stitches into one until the hole tightens and closes.

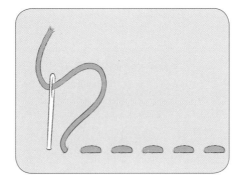

Running stitch

This is used to sew on facial features and embroider details such as noses. Bring the needle up through the fabric to the right side of the work. Working from right to left, push the needle tip in and out of the fabric at equal intervals. Do small running stitches side by side for embroidery.

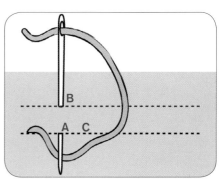

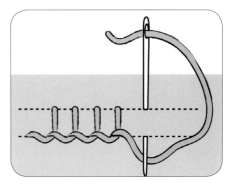

Blanket stitch

Work from left to right. Bring needle up at point A, down at B and up at C with thread looped under the needle. Pull through. Take care to tighten the stitches equally. Repeat to the right. Fasten the last loop by taking a small stitch along the lower line. When the stitch is used to join or edge, the bottom of the 'U' shape should lie on the outer edge of the fabric to form a raised line.

Sewing up

This is an important stage, as you do not want all your hard work to be ruined by the toy falling apart. Most of the stuffing and sewing up necessary for your amigurumi will be done as you go along, so there will be no need for major assembly at the end.

Sewing up is usually done using the yarn ends left when the initial magic circle is made. Using a darning needle, take small, neat stitches and try to make them show as little as possible. Fasten off yarn ends securely by taking several stitches through your work.

Abbreviations

alt	alternate	**inc**	increase
approx	approximately	**m**	metre(s)
beg	beginning	**MC**	magic circle technique
ch	chain	**mm**	millimetre(s)
cm(s)	centimetre(s)	**patt**	pattern
cont	continue	**rem**	remaining
dc	double crochet	**rep**	repeat
dc2tog	double crochet 2 sts together to decrease	**RS**	right side of work
		sl st	slip stitch
dec	decrease	**st(s)**	stitch(es)
foll	following	**tog**	together
g	gram(s)	**WS**	wrong side of work
in	inch(es)	**yd**	yard(s)

Conversions

HOOK CONVERSIONS

UK	METRIC	US
14	2mm	B/1
13	2.25mm	–
12	2.5mm	C/2
11	3mm	–
10	3.25mm	D/3
9	3.5mm	E/4
8	4mm	G/6
7	4.5mm	–
6	5mm	H/8
5	5.5mm	I/9
4	6mm	J/10

Note: check tension and use a larger/smaller hook if necessary

UK/US YARN WEIGHTS

UK	US
2-ply	Lace
3-ply	Fingering
4-ply	Sport
Double knitting	Light worsted
Aran	Fisherman/worsted
Chunky	Bulky
Super chunky	Extra bulky